PARENTING: A JOURNEY

READ THE BIBLE!

DENNIS TEYE

PARENTING PRACTITONER

PARENTING: A JOURNEY

DENNIS TEYE

PARENTING PRACTITONER

Parenting: A Journey
First published in Great Britain in 2023 by
LOTUS BOOKS
An imprint of PARTNERSHIP PUBLISHING

Written by Dennis Teye

A CIP catalogue record for this book is available from the British Library.
ISBN 978-1-915200-41-9

Book cover design by: Partnership Publishing

Book typeset by:
PARTNERSHIP PUBLISHING
North Lincolnshire, United Kingdom

www.partnershippublishing.co.uk
Printed in England

Partnership Publishing is committed to a sustainable future for our business, our readers, and our planet; an organisation dedicated to promoting responsible management of forest resources. This book is made from paper certified by the Forestry Stewardship Council (FSC) an organisation dedicated to promoting responsible management of forest resources.

We operate a distinctive and ethical publishing philosophy in all areas of our business, from our global network of Authors to production and worldwide distribution.

This book is dedicated to the parents and young people whose journeys crossed path with mine.

Special acknowledgement to my Legon Team (Ghana), Kent, Ilford, Telford and Westminster Teams (United Kingdom) and Portage (Canada)

Contents

What to Expect

Chapter 1 invites you to start thinking of parenting in a non-restrictive way. Try to view parenting beyond family, society, culture, religion, and other belief systems. The topics in this chapter can serve as an icebreaker when you want to start a discussion about parenting. These topics will help you establish if a person is objective and could be a good candidate for peer-to-peer discussions.

If you start talking to someone and they appear to be imposing their views rather than listening to you, they are probably not open to new ideas. Your goal is to keep an open mind and learn how best to offer your child a good growing up experience so that you can enjoy your role as a parent.

Chapter 2 is dedicated to discussions, debates and sharing of ideas about parenting. You can arrange to have a chat with your partner or parenting buddy on each of these topics. Agree, disagree, argue your point, and explore your reality with each topic in this chapter.

Chapter 3 is for self-evaluation. The topics in this chapter will guide you to review your upbringing and the experiences that have defined your personality. What do you know about parenting and how did you acquire this knowledge? Which aspect of your parenting needs improving?

Chapter 4 looks at some important requirements in parenting your child, a list of things that your child may need from you during their upbringing. Once you start reading this chapter, you will find that there are other things that you consider important in your child's upbringing. Talk about those, as well as the ones in this chapter.

`Chapter 5` is the concluding chapter, and it offers more topics for discussion. The interaction with others about your take on these topics is what brings this book alive. You may have other topics that you want to discuss, I hope that this book gives you the motivation and guidance to reach out to others and have those discussions.

Introduction

We do not get a manual on how to parent, but we can learn to ask for directions on our parenting journey.

The question is, "Whom do I ask for directions?" Parenting: a Journey offers the answers.
This book teaches you to master the process of asking for directions, in order to get as many answers from different people as you would if you had typed a question into an internet search engine.

Every human has experienced parenting in one form or another.

There is no better way to understand parenting than to ask others who have experienced the process. Speak to people who can give you their views and opinions using their own personal experiences. Speak to a neighbour, a friend, the person sitting next to you on the bus, or the person in the hospital waiting room.

How do I start a conversation about parenting? Start from Chapter 1, question 1.

What makes a good parent?

The Author's Journey

Phase 1 (Africa - Ghana)

My journey started in a small home where I lived with my mother and her extended family. I witnessed how my siblings were received (**their birth**) and had an insight of how poorly pregnancy out of wedlock was treated. Non-the-less, the nature of the pregnancy did not affect the welcoming and "outdooring" of the child. The outdooring or naming ceremony is a tradition of presenting the child to the world, and it is often done with honour and pride to celebrate the mother and child for surviving the pregnancy and birth.

Living with my wider family has stayed with me and I am enjoying the benefits in my adulthood, both as an individual, and a parent. I was exposed to different personalities and adult behaviours and responses. My uncles, aunties, and parents were all different, so I knew from an early age which personalities I liked and those that did not sit well with me.

Around the age of ten, we moved out of the extended family home to live as a nuclear unit with my father, two siblings and an older cousin. We went to live in an industrial city which was mainly occupied by professionals so the set up was predominantly nuclear. It was a small community, so families knew each other.

Here, I was exposed to different types of parenting styles from the various households. The father next door was different from the one two doors down and everyone knew what parenting style existed in each household. This is where the idea behind **the nature of a good parent** began. All the parents appeared to want the best for their child and to see them do well.

Education gave me a further exposure to other people's experience of parenting. I spent some time in boarding school and experienced different matrons in charge of the various accommodation units. Some of the teachers were to be feared and others were friendly but maintained their authority without the use of fear or in some cases the whip.

My time in boarding school was my first experience of how **society and others could set the agenda for a child's journey** and the parents could not do anything about it. I had friends who were introduced to illicit substances and by the time they finished their senior year in secondary school, they were addicted to illicit substances. I had been grounded by my earlier experience of living with my extended family where the negative effect of illicit substances was openly discussed.

I had an interesting experience of a teacher using the whip in anger during my secondary school years and I really questioned if there was a place in beating a child when your role is to guide and support them. Teachers could use the whip if a child turns up to school late. Some of the students travelled on public transport to school and the idea of beating someone for turning up 2 minutes late was difficult for me to accept.

During my school years, failing any of your examinations was a taboo, which signified laziness or lack of effort. The idea of helping a child to achieve a dream that a parent may have for them was not common. Failing to realise your parents dreams often led to being disliked and reminded daily how you have failed in life as a child. The irony is that often, some of the parents could not evidence what they have achieved at the time of labelling their child as a failure.

I was privileged to be guided into studying social work at university. The idea behind social work practice, which is helping the vulnerable, being the voice of the voiceless, promoting social change and challenging discrimination and abuse instantly became my goal in life.

My time at the university exposed me to a culture of travelling abroad at the end of every semester. This was when I had by first exposure to the United Kingdom and interestingly, one of my lecturers had trained in England. We often discussed the similarities and differences in child welfare between the United Kingdom and Ghana. Both countries had similar legislation, but in Ghana at the time, it was generally accepted that a parent or a teacher could pull out the whip when a child fails a test or "behaves badly".

Phase 2 - (Europe - United Kingdom)

By the end of my Bachelor's, I had fallen into a habit spending much time in England, so my first job was in London with a fostering agency. My role included recruiting, assessing, training, and supporting foster carers. In my first 6 years of practice, I had the experience of talking to couples and single carers about their experiences growing up and their understanding of parenting.

This was when the conversation started with everyone I met about parenting. My work in fostering was guided by various legislations, standards, and competencies. All of these made sense and worked well together to ensure that each foster carer who was recruited could offer a good standard of care to any child that was matched to them.

I was exposed to the background information of each foster child I met, and their journey with their birth parents. I was privileged to be part of their journey in foster care, and I saw many successful endings. I worked with foster carers to understand that **parenting ends** and supported them to help older teenagers to embrace adulthood.

I had some amazing colleagues who were experienced, intelligent, reflective, and open-minded individuals. It was a great team of people from diverse backgrounds working with foster carers from every corner of the world. I was honoured to facilitate support group sessions and it was amazing to hear experienced parents share and support each other in their individual journeys.

My next role after my fostering job was with families who needed support from their local authority. This role gave me the opportunity to work with a wide variety of families. Some of the families were open to the idea of change but others struggled to accept that they may be doing something wrong.

Having worked with foster carers who were offered training and support, I began to question why every parent is not offered the opportunity to learn parenting and have access to support groups.

I also noted that the language that was often used with families who needed support with parenting was often overwhelming and full of jargons and terminologies. For example, telling a mother who can barely read what theories and research you have used in your report. Often, these reports come across as judgemental and critical of people's parenting when the goal is to rally together and give the child the best parenting experience.

After many years of working with families who are lost in their parenting journey, I decided to find a way to engage, and have a conversation without coming across as preaching. Perhaps a way to encourage parents to find their own answers and not to feel overwhelmed by the information that they receive.

Phase 3 - (North America - Canada)

Around the time that I started thinking of how to put the idea of "good enough parenting" into a conversation with the parent, I migrated to Canada. After working with Families for 14 years in the private and public sector in England, I did not expect the wealth of experience and learning opportunity that I was presented with in my next role.

I went to work in a substance misuse rehabilitation center. The youngest age that was accepted for residential treatment was thirteen and there was no limit, as some retirees and grandparents checked in for 6 months to address their alcohol dependency so that they **could at least have a second chance with a grandchild.**

It was a delight to work with both the young and old in their recovery. It was refreshing to see people in treatment persevere, build resilience, understand their struggles, and take charge of their recovery.

This was a real-life experience of observing individuals work as part of a team to understand the reason behind their substance misuse. Working in this environment came with many reading opportunities, access, and exposure to experts in the field of trauma and addiction.

I was able to see how the parenting journey caused many problems to the individuals who came in for treatment. Issues arising from parenting in isolation, child labelling, lack of understanding of additional needs, and parents who were lost on their journey.

I observed how the lack of opportunity to understand and learn about parenting caused pain which then resulted in people trying to alleviate the pain with alcohol, drugs, and behaviours that were self-destructive.
I came to understand how the pain often caused people to isolate themselves and lose the opportunity to get support in their various journeys in life.

One of my roles was to offer support to parents of the teenagers through weekly support groups. As I observed individuals in treatment discover themselves and understand the causes of the pain that led them to addiction, I was able to hear their parents account of their journeys together.

The life story according to the parent and the child's version of how they felt. The legacy that parents were planning without knowing what the reality was for the child. **Giving your child everything and yet leaving them with nothing.**

When the parents came together in a support group meeting, they were able to lift each other's spirit. The opportunity to explore and understand their own experience of parenting, the opportunity to learn what really matters in parenting and the forum to share ideas with others about their journey.

Phase 4 - (Here and now)

It has been a while since my journey started. I have taken on much baggage along the way, precious purchases, impulsive acquisition, some reckless choices, and many others I cannot even remember.

As I reflect on my parenting decisions and the choices I have made, I am proud to take full responsibility for my accomplishment and of course accept that there is room for improvement.

My journey as a child was a blast and my adult life has been fulfilling. I have lived in three worlds, three lifetimes in one existence. I have been privileged to have met and learnt from many and I want to share.

I am enjoying my journey as a parent and continue to live and reflect on my day-to-day choices. This book is part of my search for a library of resources as part of my journey. This is my conversation with you, with the world to find out what everyone thinks about the nature of a good parent. This is me asking you if we should be talking to each other as parents.

I am human, yet I am perfect in my own special way, and I believe that if I continue to engage with others, I will continue to improve as a parent.

The competition is with myself, and I wish to improve on my record. I will keep aiming to better my best achievements.

This is my parenting journey.

Why This Book?

After two decades of working with families on three continents, I have come to understand that every parent can do a good job when given the right guidance and support. Parents generally repeat what they know, from feeding a baby to teaching a child how to hunt. Mistakes can be made, and some choose to do their own thing, but our basic instincts mostly cause us to repeat learnt behaviour.

Parenting knowledge has, over the centuries, been passed down through communities of people. As we focus more on our nuclear families, we neglect the opportunity to learn as a community. This has made the parenting journey an isolated experience for many people.

The idea behind Parenting: a Journey is to encourage you to take advantage of the resources and information available to you along the way. If you accept that almost every human has experienced parenting, in one form or another, won't it be easier to get as many people as possible to give you ideas on how to offer your child the best parenting experience?

I have facilitated many parenting groups, and what is remarkable about these meetings is that when people start talking, they tend to provide each other with the answers they are looking for, with very little professional guidance.

The professional guidance is often asking people the right question and giving them the space to discuss and find their own answers.

After reading each topic in this book, I encourage you to talk to a friend or your partner and ask them what they think. There will be many discussions and good opinions but remember that every person you speak to will give you their point of view. This means that you cannot settle for the first or second opinion, you need a lot more. These different perspectives are what will help you on your parenting journey, so that when you are faced with a situation, you have ten to twenty suggestions to help you decide on the correct course of action.

Before Birth

If an unborn child could make a wish, he (or she) would ask for an open-minded parent with a big heart.

Chapter 1

An overview of parenting

Find out what others think about certain topics when it comes to parenting.

Ask them the questions in this chapter or tell them about the book and ask them to comment on the discussion provided.

Part 1: The Nature of Good Parenting

What makes a 'good' parent?

Your main role as a parent is to ensure that your child is suitably fed and kept safe. Life often throws challenges in our way. However, if you are genuinely trying to do the best by your child, that is the nature of good parenting.

Good parenting is the ongoing attempt to provide the basic requirements for a child with the single aim of ensuring that every decision made about their upbringing is appropriate for their current and future wellbeing.
Good parenting is being spontaneous yet disciplined in your care for a child.
Good parenting is making sensible choices and not blindly following a social trend.
Good parenting is taking a stand for a child and not allowing friends, family, or society to set the agenda.
Good parenting is being confident in yourself and not worrying about what others may say or think because you place importance on what is best for your child.
Good parenting is knowing that there will be many challenges along the way but being prepared to fix things and continue learning.

Part 2: Identity

How does my identity impact on my parenting?

Our heritage and identity often form the foundation of our lifestyles and parenting choices. Every human society has its own culture, tradition, and belief systems. It is upon these that most people formulate their parenting styles and understanding of child development.

Some parenting methods that are prescribed by one group are not accepted by another. For example, there is often a debate on the use of smacking in parenting. One of the arguments that is put across is that sometimes a parent may smack their child excessively causing them harm. Some talk about a gentle tap on the back of the hand and others something different.

There are instances where parenting practices are unacceptable due to the health or psychological impact on a child. Despite the opposition, some parents often argue that it is their culture, and they continue regardless.

We can all agree that it is important to promote and support our heritage and the traditions that come with them. Unfortunately, sometimes our quest to promote or preserve traditions have cost our societies dearly. Sometimes, we can misinterpret or misrepresent our own culture and tradition without realizing our mistakes.

Knowing your heritage and following your traditions can give you a sense of purpose in life. On the contrary, if we do not know who we are, Identity crisis can leave us empty and confused about ourselves. Our culture and traditions serve as a guide on our parenting journey.

On the topic of parenting, there is one fundamental rule; the child's welfare should come first. If your culture, tradition, or belief system interferes with your ability to keep your child safe, then you need to find out the reasoning behind those traditions. Our societies are not as they were thousands of years ago; you can make the necessary adjustments for your child and perhaps your community.

It is okay to belong to a group of people and still choose what is best for your child.

Part 3: Humanity

How will my parenting affect others?

Regardless of your reasons for having a child, your child is a member of a wider community. They can populate the world, care for you in your old age and be an important contributor to their community.

Your parenting will ultimately determine the future of another human being. In other words, how you parent your child will impact their friends, family, and humanity.

It is individuals like you and your child who have worked together to build cities and nations.

Humanity requires you to be a 'good' parent so that your child will add to what our predecessors have started. As a parent, you will be in an important position when raising your child. The parenting choices and decisions you make could give the world a happy person, a good parent or someone who is excelling in their chosen trade or career.

If you fail to provide your child with the appropriate care and nurturing, they require, you may prevent them from achieving their true potential.

Poor parenting could unnecessarily cause a child to become dependent rather than contribute to society.

Getting it right for your child may be your way of contributing to society. A child who has been brought up 'right', such as benefitting from a supportive parent, could have direct or indirect input in something important for a group, society, or the world. They could simply be law-abiding citizens and get on with their lives.

Part 4: Teaching

What can I teach my child?

Teaching is an important part of parenting, and it even happens unconsciously. You begin to teach your child human interaction from the minute they are born. This includes how you respond to them when they need feeding or changing. As the months pass, you introduce your child to certain foods and teach them to accept different tastes and texture of food. The opportunity to teach a child is limitless.

Parenting offers you the **privilege** to teach your child about life. Bear in mind that you have limitations in terms of what you know. It is fair to say that you are better in some subjects than others. In other words, you do not know everything.

Your child may finish learning certain things from you by 'age nine' depending on how much you have to offer them on a subject. For example, the parent who is not gifted in mathematics knows when to leave their child to get on with their math homework or ask someone else for help.

Learn in your role as a parent and do not get comfortable with the little you know. It is okay not to know much and use your parenting journey to learn along with your child. Do not act like you know everything, **treat parenting as a journey and ask for directions along the way.**

Be careful not to misinform your child as a parent. Your child may take in everything that you teach them as factual even when it is not. This may continue in their adult life and when they meet a partner who has a different or perhaps a better view, they will insist that their mother or father is always correct.

Having all the answers without knowing the questions is dangerous in any field of life.

Part 5: Titles

What title do I wear as a parent?

The parenting title is one of the most prevalent on the earth as it often comes easy on the surface. It is generally accepted that having a child makes you a parent regardless of where the child may be, or your contribution towards the child's life.

The issue of misplaced titling is not unique to parenting as there are examples of men proposing, and attending their wedding ceremony, but having no intention to fulfil the role a of husband. The same could be true for a man or woman who spends years planning their special day even before the partner comes along but does not take the time to find out what the role of a wife or husband entails.

Some people are not fortunate and through no fault of theirs, do not get the opportunity to parent their child. However, planning for a child and having one does not make you a parent. You need to practice parenting by caring for that child.

If a person has no intention to embark on the parenting journey when they have every opportunity to do so, their child may inadvertently see them differently from what they may perceive of themselves. Your child may see you as a financial provider and even worse, some parents have been referred to as sperm donors or surrogates.

A child needs clarity about the responsibilities of a father and a mother because what you teach them now is what they will aspire to be when they grow up. It is confusing when a child sees other fathers doing the opposite to the man whom their mother tells them to call “daddy”.

Your focus as a parent is to teach the right thing and making excuses for an absent parent is inappropriate. Do not misinform your child, help them to understand the roles and responsibilities of a parent, male or female.

Part 6: Expectations

What do I expect of my child?

Age is often overlooked when dealing with a child who does not do as expected.

For example, the two-year-old who is starting to shout back words and repeat things such as "pick me up", "thank you" and "sorry" is doing trial and error learning. If a parent sees this two-year-old heading for the fireplace, "stop it and do not touch" will be a trial- and-error instruction. You are literally playing with fire as a parent if you do not make the effort to physically prevent the child from getting burnt. You need to teach the child not to touch fire and "do not touch" or "it is hot" may be how you teach them, but this will take time to register.

If an eight-year-old swears at an adult, the adult assumes the child is disrespectful. Yes, the language is inappropriate, but the question is, what else is wrong with this scenario? Other behaviours may cause an adult to think that the child does not demonstrate certain fundamental values such as honesty. When dealing with a child, if something happens and you feel that it is out of the ordinary, identify the first wrong then explore if there is anything else that is not right about the situation. Always bear in mind that you are dealing with a child.

Once you start thinking of your child's poor behaviour as a difficulty for them, you will shift to describing them as unexpected rather than inappropriate behaviours. Your focus will be on asking questions to identify the real issue and not vilifying your child any time you are faced with **unexpected behaviour.**

Do not use the adult justice system on your child. There is a good reason why we have a separate youth justice system and why there is no justice system for toddlers.

Part 7: Behaviour Management

How do I manage my child's behaviour?

Behaviour management is a key topic in parenting but when the need arises to explore this matter, people automatically assume the child is the problem.

The two-year-old who is seen as badly behaved has only been here 24 months and is still trying to pick up words, understand humans, and train to use the toilet.

Then there's the 4-week-old baby who cries all the time and their mother or father wants the child to stop "that behaviour". It could even be the 16-year-old whose behaviour is described by their teacher as 'appalling'.

If these three were siblings and a couple wanted to adopt or care for them temporarily, the expectation would be on the adult rather than the child. Before the couple are considered to care for the siblings, a trained professional would spend several months finding out about the couple's individual childhood experiences, their relationships, educational experience, physical health, mental health and their understanding of any issues that these siblings may have. Special training may be offered to help the prospective parent understand child development and behaviour management.

This approach appears to be widely accepted by professionals and society in general yet with birth families, little emphasis is placed on the parents' background, their skills, or their understanding of how to manage a child's behaviour.

If there is an adult and a child living in a house and things are not going well, who has a better understanding of the world and can make sensible changes to minimise the impact on the family? A 16-year-old has never been a teenager whereas their parent has been there and also gained adulthood experience.

A parent can make decisions, choices, learn or seek help from others to address or balance things at home. A child does not have these privileges, nor do they have any life experiences to fall back on.

Part 8: Expert Advice

What is good parenting advice?

Childbirth does not guarantee appropriate parenting skills. Parenting is a never-ending cycle of learning, and the list of **frequently asked questions** grows as human societies evolve.

Many 'experts' explain the child/parent relationship as if they are relating to subordinates and a manager in the workplace. If the child does not do as expected, the parent needs to put disciplinary measures in place to stop the bad behaviour.

When raising your child, others will be able to interfere in the work that you are doing. It is your responsibility to best manage any negative impact from the outside.

If your child's behaviour is inappropriate, unless there are health or developmental issues, something has gone wrong on the parenting journey. For example, a two-year-old using abusive language must have heard that language from you or someone else.

How do you solve the two-year old's inappropriate language issue? This question should only be answered after taking time to understand the bigger picture. It should not be a straightforward "discipline" the child and tell them it is naughty or to stop.

If parenting was that simple, our societies would have little need for law enforcement officials in our adult lives. In addition to helping the child delete the word from their language in your own effective way, do investigate who or where they may be hearing such language. Your "stop it" may not work if your child continues to be exposed to bad language.

It is critical to understand the origin of an issue in order to apply the appropriate solution.

Part 9: Child Labelling

Do I label my child?

There appears to be no widely accepted criteria in identifying a badly-behaved child. A child is often punished for his actions when often he or she needs help, an assessment to understand what is going on, or simply to be accepted for who they are.

There are situations where a child is labelled as being 'badly behaved' due to a lack of understanding on the parents' part. In some cases, a child's 'normal' behaviour becomes an issue in their parents' eyes. For example, let's take a child who is more active than average. Some parents may be inclined to 'fix' their child when they should work to meet their child's active needs by providing opportunities, such as an organised sport, for the child to use his or her energy.

It may be that the child has a medical condition, and the parent is not aware. Therefore, instead of taking the child to the doctor, the parent conveniently slaps the 'bad behaviour' label on them. The parent then proceeds to find a way to address the issues and this is often the punishment approach. One such example is a child whose bedwetting is a result of a condition called Enuresis. Telling that child to stop bedwetting and threatening them is not likely to address a psychological or medical issue. It simply adds a layer of worry to their existing condition.

Some behaviours are caused by social or environmental issues. In these situations, the child is a victim rather than the villain. A child who is constantly being shouted at or witnessing domestic abuse at home may become withdrawn and struggle to concentrate at school. This may result in disruptive or violent behaviour, which is inappropriate but, given the bigger picture, the child could be described as crying for help.

Part 10: Practicing Parenting

Is my parenting style working for my child?

What happens when you give parenting instructions or advice to someone who does not know how to apply them? Getting a manual or instruction with something you purchased does not always guarantee that you can successfully apply them. Some may take a long time but eventually figure it out, but others may simply not understand.

Spend some time learning about parenting, perhaps 30 minutes a day or a couple of hours to reflect on what you are doing. If you feel that it is a bit too much for you, get help. Let someone else start it for you or even do it for you. Your goal is to put things in order and help your child, not to win a challenge.

Seek effective behaviour managing techniques and methods that have consistently worked and are supported by experts and other parents. However, finding the solution or answer to a difficulty that you have with your child does not guarantee you can address the issue. If it is not working, please refrain from blaming your child. You should look at yourself: are you doing it right?

Child development or growing up involves several complex changes in the human body. This often makes parenting look like an impossible task and even the most experienced and open-minded individuals sometimes struggle to get the balance right.

If you are genuinely trying despite the challenges and you have left no stone unturned, keep going. Your goal is not to win the challenge but to give your child the best that you can offer.

Chapter 2

Parenting discussion 1

Ask others what they think about the discussions in this chapter.

Start your own list of topics that you want to discuss. Share your views with others and ask them to share theirs.

Speak to many people for different perspectives.

Part 1: Relationships

How do I build a relationship with my child?

Think back to the first day that you met your child. You had a vision of how you wanted your relationship to be with your child. Loving, caring, respectful, loyal, truthful, trustworthy, and many other positive attributes that are associated with human relationships.

Let us imagine this relationship is with a partner. When you meet for the first time, you take things slowly and learn about each other. You make the effort to build the relationship and continue to learn and get to know each other to improve on things as the years go by. This is what you expect for two adults who already know about life and what they need to do in a relationship.

Back to the child at the labour ward. Do we think about dedicating time and effort to building a relationship, or do we expect maternal and paternal intuition or instincts to lead the way? Often, parents do not think of their relationship with the child as one that requires the same level of effort that they will put into other partnerships. Perhaps the relationship with the child requires more effort because only the adult has life experience and prior knowledge of how to form a relationship.

How then does the child learn to be loving, caring, respectful, loyal, trustworthy, and truthful in your relationship with them? To achieve these goals in your relationship with a child, a parent needs to have these qualities, be willing and able to live them, teach them and be patient to allow room for error.

In the adult world, many spend years together with the desire, hope, and drive to build a healthy relationship only to give up because one or both parties are not able to achieve what they desire.

Every relationship requires time and effort to develop, it does not happen by chance. Your relationship with your child is not different, it needs work and time to develop.

Part 2: Couples

How does my relationship impact on my child?

To be able to offer a stable and stimulating environment, a couple with a child in their care must first understand and appreciate their relationship goals. They must be willing and able to welcome another individual into their relationship. How the couple manage their relationship will be both a living and learning experience for the child.

A couple must not find themselves constantly patching things. It is okay to fix a problem here and there as expected in every human relationship but **saying that every relationship has its difficulty should not be said too often.**

Being sensitive to your partner's needs promotes a strong relationship. This means knowing their strengths and weaknesses, habits, behaviour, reactions, responses, their dreams, and goals in life.

If you love somebody and you have done the work to build a relationship, everything falls in place naturally. You will find that your focus will not be on whether they love you but rather on enjoying each other and making each other happy.

Your child needs this exposure to learn about couples and parenting with another person. There are many instances where people stay in relationships unhappy for personal reasons. Looking from the outside, it may not look right but our lives are not without challenges and dare I say, complications. The good news is that couples do disagree and sometimes overstep their own boundaries, but ideally, couples should not engage in physical altercations.

Part 3: Siblings

How do I parent siblings?

Having more than one child and seeing them develop a healthy relationship is refreshing and rewarding. Parenting more than one child comes with benefits but also some challenges. For many, having more than one child is what they deem as a complete family while others prefer one child.

Your experiences as a child and the knowledge you acquired in your adult years will form the basis of your decision making as a parent. If you have no experience or exposure to raising siblings, it is best to learn before the task becomes a crisis within your household. Expect more challenges in terms of decision making, unexpected events, friendship issues, and personality differences or similarities.

Your sibling group of two should be treated as unique, encouraged to look out for each other's safety and be honest with one another. If you have two boys, they must not be expected to automatically treat each with respect, they must be taught. You may use the discussion on safety in Chapter 4, Part 3 to ensure that appropriate measures are taught or put in place to keep them safe both as individuals and as siblings.

You may have a sibling group and find that one is thriving and the other seems to be struggling. Trying to help the struggling child is inevitable but do not do it at the expense of the other. You may have a situation where siblings do not get along, but the focus should remain on their individual needs, teamwork will happen naturally if they receive appropriate support and all the requirements stated in Chapter 4 are prioritised in their individual care.

You cannot build a team when you do not have competent and well supported individual players.

Part 4: Parenting Issues

How do I manage parenting issues?

The day-to-day care of a child does not lend itself to careful planning. On the contrary, having the time to make it this far in this book is a commendable achievement for most parents given the demands that their child places on their everyday life.

If your childhood experiences were poor and you have not had any positive role modelling in your life, then sharing a home with your child will take some time to master. Parents are quick to point fingers at the child for being badly behaved when they have no idea how to address a simple issue.

Take the example of a baby that cries each time it needs to be fed. To start with, ask yourself: 'how do I address this issue?' The answer should not be what the child must or should not do. As the parent, you could take note of how often the baby needs to be fed and plan ahead.

If you lack basic parenting skills, the simplest of chores will present as a huge task. For example, a parent who is trying to get a child into a routine starting from when they wake up, through mealtimes to bedtime may struggle and find this a painful experience if they don't have any prior experience or knowledge of how to go about it.

Seek help to achieve your objective. Use individuals, books, professionals, or any appropriate means of learning. The objective is to learn, and the plan should reflect your circumstance. Address any knowledge gaps to prevent avoidable parenting issues.

Part 5: Additional Requirements (special needs)

How do I manage if my child is different?

Our societies have come up with several different labels and titles to describe special needs (additional care needs). Some of these titles are well researched and appropriate support is in place to help any child who displays the need for assistance. Some form of assessment or evaluation is required to be able to understand and offer appropriate support. It is not always possible to understand some of the additional requirements that a child may present.

The more recognisable and widely accepted additional requirements are often categorised under child mental health. Despite being well researched and resourced, it is difficult to be the parent whose child needs psychiatric or psychological support. These needs can range from mild to severe and may present in many forms.

You are one of the fortunate ones if your child has access to services and they have a diagnosis that appears to be the right one. Many are missed and therefore miss out on the opportunity to be treated and others are unfortunately misdiagnosed. Some spend years trying to understand how to help their child and not everyone is successful. This affects the child and their parents at various stages of life and in different ways.

It is not unusual to have a situation where parents blame their poor parenting skills on the child. Some go as far as seeking professional help for their child and advocating for a diagnosis to validate their perceptions. Some do not acknowledge that their child may have some additional needs and refuse any form of intervention.

Having special needs is not a life sentence. In many situations, a diagnosis offers the child and parent a path to a better quality of life.

Part 6: Personal Development

How do I continue to develop as a parent?

Your birth family or life experiences may not have equipped you with the necessary skills or knowledge to be able to offer your child the level of care that is appropriate for them.

Personal development in parenting may often take the form of unlearning and this is particularly the case for many parents who were brought up in an abusive and oppressive environment. Take for example some of the topics discussed in Chapter 3, your childhood experience of parenting. Without seeking to develop as a parent, how would you know that your understanding of most things is wrong? Lacking patience and being hot-tempered is not something that disappears with age or the birth of your child, it takes some form of learning to first accept that you have a problem that needs to be addressed.

Uniqueness, honesty, money, safety and other subjects that you deem are important for your child to learn may not necessarily be areas where you know well. As the days go by, topics such as money and safety take different forms. Safety and money these days include online predators as well as identity theft which was not the case a few years back.

Your child's care needs may require you to be open-minded about your personal development. If you find that your child is a step ahead or two steps behind developmentally, then you may need to keep up otherwise the child may take over the steering wheel on the parenting journey and you will become a passenger instead of being the driver.

Keep in mind that there may be one or more aspects of parenting where you did not have a good learning experience from your parents. **Be willing and open to the idea of improving your parenting.**

Part 7: Parenting Mistakes

What is acceptable as a parenting mistake?

Parenting comes with several challenges and some people are ill equipped to rise to these resulting in undesired experiences for both parent and child. Many parents view themselves as the authority in their child's life. That is, all-knowing and flawless. The notion of being flawless as a parent is particularly true for people who do not understand their role or place in a child's life. Our lives cannot always be planned but repeating a parenting technique that has not worked for your first child with the second is an example of parenting mistakes that should be avoided.

You may experience struggles in life or have to deal with challenges but as long as your child remains a priority, you are fulfilling your duty as a parent. You may unknowingly repeat some mistakes which unfortunately are part of your upbringing, and this can be distressing for both you and the child. You may shout, get angry, and use inappropriate techniques to feed, over chastise, or even get physical. A parent may break the law with their child and receive a criminal sentence due to their own parenting experiences or because they do not understand their child's additional needs.

Poor parenting behaviour can only be described as a mistake if you try to avoid a repeat. You have a short window as a parent to get it right before your child becomes a young adult.

If you only realise that it is not appropriate to slap your son when he is 14 years old, that is 77% of his childhood gone. For the remaining 23% of his childhood, you may have a difficult time teaching him that a parent should not slap their son every day.

When you make a mistake, acknowledge it, and let your child know that it is not the right thing to do. Then you can proceed to do what is right and make it a learning opportunity for your child on their journey with you.

Part 8: Age Range

What age child do I feel more comfortable to parent?

When a childcare professional is given the option to choose an age group to work with, they identify the ages that they feel most confident to support. Teachers, nurses, foster carers, doctors, babysitters, and many others are specific when asked about the age range they want to provide care for as professionals.

Many of these professionals arrive at their decision after carefully evaluating their practice and dealings with zero- to eighteen-year-olds. A nursery teacher may not enjoy working with teenagers as much as they enjoy caring for babies. Likewise, a foster carer who prefers teenagers may not enjoy waking up in the middle of the night to check on a new-born baby. There are however professionals who are comfortable with all ages, and they seem to do well.

In comparing the professional approach of the age range to parenting, one can say that there are parents who are comfortable with a child regardless of their age and others who prefer a specific age. You may identify a specific period of your child's life where you feel that you were at your best as a parent.

The discussion on identifying your best age range is to promote awareness. Once you become aware of the age you are most comfortable with, you will be able to seek support when necessary or acknowledge that you are the one struggling, and the child is not being difficult. This approach is important to identify family and friends to support you at the ages where you are less confident as a parent.

Part 9: Moving On

How do I make the right decision for my child?

Making the decision to leave an abusive partner who may be putting you and your child at risk of serious injuries is not an easy decision for a parent to make. Sometimes the child may have a good relationship with the abuser, and this does not make the decision any easier. Many abusers, criminals, offenders, and murderers are oblivious to their actions and the plight of their victims. A parent needs to make the decision to move on from any situation that compromises their own and their child's safety, whether it is physical violence or any of form of inappropriate behaviour.

It is toxic to hold on to issues from the past when the accused has modified their ways. However, **it is unwise to forgive someone every week for being offensive or abusive towards you.** The fact that they are your partner, parent or they support you financially does not right their wrongs. **If you would not tolerate a certain behaviour from an outsider, it is not appropriate for someone who loves you to do that to you**. Good people do not make a habit of doing bad things to their loved ones. Your child may either copy your response or live in fear of your plight.

Unfortunately, advocates in some societies may encourage victims to compromise for the sake of their marriage. Moving on is not a decision that comes easy, especially if there are financial constraints or if the act of leaving places the person at a higher risk. If you are in the position to move on, this could signify the beginning of your adult life or a fresh start for you to provide that stable environment for your child to thrive. If possible, get a professional or someone who has no link to the situation to help you. Avoid individuals who have all the answers; you need people who can empower you to find your own answers.

If you are not able to move on at this point in your life, do not be too hard on yourself. If, despite life's challenges, you are genuinely trying, that is the nature of good parenting.

Part 10: Letting Go

What if I cannot parent my child?

Some people accept that parenting is not for them and as such refrain from having a child. Some will give a child away because they feel that they are not ready to be parents. These individuals or couples are often ridiculed and looked down upon as if they have committed a crime.

The nature of good parenting does not mean that you should always have a child in your care. Good parenting is taking a stand for your child and not allowing friends, family or society to set the agenda for you. Good parenting is being confident in yourself and not worrying about what others may say or think about you as you place importance on what is best for your child.

If you are unable to care for your child and you have to allow someone else to do so (temporarily or permanently), you are being selfless and looking out for your child's interests. However, if you've had to give up one or two children and you proceed to fall pregnant or you get another woman pregnant when you cannot provide for your first child, this is irresponsible.

Giving up a child is not something that most parents would ever consider. A parent may have the will power and genuinely try their best, but life can sometimes be harsh. If you have to let go temporarily, do not hesitate. If you cannot parent, remember a child's life is at stake. This is a tough decision that may require support from others. Avoid those who are ignorant about your circumstances or the subject matter.

Letting go may be the best decision that you could make for your child's upbringing. This decision might give your child the chance to a healthy and happy childhood where they are safe from harm.

Chapter 3

Your experience of parenting

Someone took you on the parenting journey as a child, what was your experience? Would you use the same route?

Ask others about their journey and share your experience with them.

Part 1: My Birth

How was I received into the world?

When you have a child to raise, you need to understand how you were received and the type of bond that you had with your parents. This will help you identify whether you need to seek help or pay closer attention to your relationship building with your child. You need to understand how your parents felt when you were born and how those feelings may have impacted on their parenting of you.

In some cultures, and societies, a child born out of wedlock is still not received well as compared to having a child in a relationship. The stigma and rebuke that the parent suffers could impact the parent-child relationship. If the parent is not emotionally strong or supported by others, they may spend the child's early years worrying about other people's views and not focus on bonding with the baby.

There are other situations where a parent may not be happy with the birth of their child for personal reasons. For example, unplanned pregnancy or having a girl instead of a boy or vice versa. A parent who is unhappy about the birth of their child may miss the opportunity to build a close bond during the early and important years of the child's life. This may have an impact on how the child learns to build relationships.

If your childhood experience is that of rejection and constant resentment, it is essential to know how it impacts your ability to build relationships. For example, if you grew up in a household where every child that came along was not welcomed, how would you know there is another way to receive a child? You may not notice the impact, but this could affect your relationship with your child.

Part 2: My Upbringing

How was I raised?

If you were fortunate to have parents who cared for you and provided all your day-to-day requirements, you are likely to repeat this or even try to make things better for your child. On the other hand, if your parents did not do their best by you, you may repeat their mistakes. Sometimes these mistakes may be habits or behaviours that you picked up outside your home. The truth is, if you do not get the opportunity to experience what is right, you may not know it exists.

Our experiences have an impact on us, but they do not always determine who we become as adults. The point of interest here is knowing where you came from and where you want to go.

Review your childhood so that you can identify and address any mistakes your parents made. This will help to ensure that your child has a positive experience. Share you experience with others and ask them to tell you about theirs. This may be how you find out the alternative or the right way of raising a child.

If you grew up in a society where a woman's only aspiration is to get married and have a family, it will take a lot of discussions with others to appreciate the important contribution of women in the world.

If you are unaware of your upbringing, you may end up in an "auto parent mode" and just repeat what you experienced. You may have a clever girl child who could be a high achiever and not support her in school.

When you take time to review your upbringing, you will be able to reflect on the parenting techniques that do not sit well with you and seek a remedy so that your child will have a better parenting experience.

Review - Reflect - Remedy

Part 3: Social Interaction

What is my experience interacting with people?

Social awareness or social interaction skills are key features that a parent needs to teach a child. It must be highlighted that there are instances where people have difficulty with social interaction due to a mental health condition. Poor social interaction skills does not always limit a person's achievement in life. A person may not understand how society works but still have a "successful career".

You may feel that you do not have any friends or people you would consider "real friends" or perhaps you struggle with keeping your partners and you are beginning to accept that everyone leaves eventually. This does not mean that people do not like you. It may be that you struggle to keep these relationships going.

Taking time to understand your background may help you identify where this came from and how it is affecting your relationships. This may not be something that you can solve on your own so seeking a professional's opinion or support may be necessary.

Your poor social interaction skills could impact your relationship with your child.

Imagine being the child whose parent is not able to sustain a relationship.

Wherever you stand, get help to address this issue and find the middle ground for your child to learn what is right. If you have a diagnosis which impacts on your social interaction, get support with your parenting, and take care of yourself.

Part 4: Emotions

What is my experience and understanding of emotions?

Our emotions impact our thought processes, decision making and actions. Our emotions determine whether we are happy or sad, content or dissatisfied, and ultimately how we feel about ourselves and those around us. Our emotions are **a medium of universal communication.** Emotions speak to us and tell others about us. **No wonder the message of love is conveyed via our emotions.**

Becoming a parent means that you are going to start using more of this medium of universal communication. This is how your child will communicate with you in their early days until they can process and fully understand language. If a parent does not understand the impact of their emotions on their child, they run the risk of causing a lot of damage. Nonetheless, a child needs to be exposed to their parents' emotions in order to understand their own and learn how to respond and manage them properly.

There are many individuals who live with the negative impacts of their parents' emotional presence in their lives. This can present various behavioural or psychological challenges and may not always be traced back to the cause.

What is your understanding of emotions? Any negative perspective that you may have in regard to emotions could have an effect on your parenting. Are you able to identify how you are feeling and act appropriately? Are you able to relate to people emotionally? Do you understand yours and others' emotions? These are some of the questions you should be answering to ensure that you can help your child rather than hurt them emotionally.

Part 5: Decision Making

What was my childhood experience of decision making?

Did you grow up in a home where your parents gave instructions with no option to discuss or understand why? Then you may have missed a learning opportunity. While you engage in decision making as a parent, the aim is that you teach your child the process of making and arriving at decisions.

Probably more than any profession on earth, parenting involves making many decisions. You may be struggling to make good parental decisions compared to your work. This is not unusual. You studied or trained for your profession, and in most cases, there is guidance in the form of policies and procedures to follow. There are no such guidelines when it comes to parenting.

When you look back and reflect on your upbringing, you will be able to understand how decision making occurred and the impact it had on you then and now. If decision making is chaotic and inconsistent, it often leads to disorganisation and life becomes unpredictable and uncomfortable. When decision making is good, it adds to a child's experience of appropriate parenting, and this enriches their early years while preparing them for their adulthood.

If you are a single parent and you realise that you are not gifted with making sound decisions, educate yourself, get help or learn from someone and seek appropriate support for your child. In the case of couples, work together. It can work well when a child knows that they have to refer to one parent when it comes to decisions. It is not a problem to say, "let's check with your mother or father" occasionally or every time you need to make a decision.

Part 6: The Unexpected

How was I taught to respond to the unexpected or undesired?

Life does not always lend us the opportunity to plan and even when things are planned, and we know what the outcome may be, it does not always work out. Parenting is no different and even more difficult to predict how a child may behave.

Let us look at two scenarios: getting a telephone call from school to report that your child has broken his friend's nose; going home to find that your child has broken your television set. Both instances trigger a reaction, and this is where a child learns from the adult.

Breaking the television should naturally be less upsetting than hearing that another child had been hospitalised due to your child's actions. Your child may copy your response as this may be the first time they are faced with such situations. Therefore, a parent's reaction must be appropriate and proportional to the situation at hand and not extreme or highly misplaced.

Your experience as a child on how to handle the unexpected will have an impact on how you respond to things in your adult life. When you become a parent, you will expose your child to your responses. Your child is learning from you; they are looking to you to show them the way. You may show disapproval and disappointment in several ways but bear in mind that no matter what the situation is, your child is learning.

Consequences, punishment, and reprimands need to be carefully thought through to ensure that a child learns from their mistakes rather than suffer for their mistakes.

Part 7: Passion

What is my understanding of passion in parenting?

We all have something or someone we consider special. Passion is what drives us to act and respond unconditionally. In other words, **passion aids the expression of love, the drive to learn, earn, achieve, and it promotes the development of talent and special skills.** Passion can be understood by others or sometimes make no sense to the people around you.

It is worth highlighting that passion is not always a positive feature as someone's idea of passion may harm themselves or others. For example, having the passion to break into people's homes and steal their property is not worth celebrating. There is also the issue of overindulging in one's passion or taking to something that impacts negatively on a person's quality of life, for example, speeding or stunt driving on a public road.

If your parents encouraged you to have passion for something such as a sport, music, dance, literature, shoes, a profession, friendship, or a pet, it is likely that you picked one and are enjoying the benefits. For example, you may have season ticket for a basketball or football team, and you make sure that watching their games is your self-love moment.

Your child is going to be exposed to a world where people have passion for things and they dedicate time, effort and in some cases a lot of money to funding their passion. You cannot dismiss your child's passion or love for something because you do not share that passion. You have to invest in teaching your child to enjoy life, learn about passion and ultimately do something they enjoy.

Part 8: Friendships

How did my parents support my friendships?

Understanding your childhood friendships could help you make sense of your child's. Your child's friendships may be positive, and it will be good to support them. However, if you find that their friendships are potentially putting them at risk of harm, take the necessary steps to keep them safe.

A child or young person may form friendships out of their own free will or be guided by their parent and this relationship may benefit both parties. Parents need to know what is going on with their child’s friendships. If everything seems fine, then it probably is. Do not become an investigative detective in your child’s friendships; it is not difficult to find out if things are not right.

It is easy to assume that your child's friendships are not important if your experience of friendships is negative, for example if they led you to try illicit substances or engage in criminal behaviour. Use your experience as a lesson to prevent your child from making the same mistakes. Do not shut your child away from the outside world, support and supervise them when they make friends.

Our friends and family are ultimately the people who become our support network. Do not limit your child's chances of having a strong network of support in the future. Use your own experience as the guide to help your child have positive peer relationships.

Part 9: Aspirations

What did my parents want me to be?

It is quite common for a parent to want their child to follow in their footsteps. This accounts for many fathers passing on their names and sons taking up their father's trade.

It is admirable that a parent may have high hopes and aspirations for their child, but the outcome depends entirely on a child's natural abilities and how they are brought up. Some believe that we all have the potential to be high achievers. This view is far from reality.

Some parents are liberal about their expectations, but others refuse to accept anything less from their child. It is "**Dad's way**", or you will be reminded every day of your life that you are a failure and a disgrace to the family name. Often when the child rejects a parent's dream, the parent turns against their child thereby causing the child to have a difficult and unhappy life.

Using the education system may not always be an accurate measure of your child's true potential. Some may need directing but others tend to discover their talent at an early age.

Your child can become successful in life, but the teacher alone cannot get them there.

If you want to make a man out of your son, be a man and do what is right by contributing to their journey.

You may have grown up in an environment different from your child or you may have different aspirations. Either way, it is vital to understand and accept the circumstances and treat your child as an individual. If they do not have any aspirations, keep supporting them to at least become law abiding citizens who can contribute to society.

Part 10: Feedback

What will my child say about their experience of parenting?

Imagine a world where every parent is given feedback about their performance by their child who is now an adult. All these aspects of parenting which you may not have paid close attention to until reading this book.

Topics such as promoting and supporting your child's passion, decision making, friendship, social interaction and others that may spring to mind while reading this chapter. Will you be keen to hear what your child will say about their experience of growing up?

As you embark on your parenting journey, one of the things that is helpful in keeping parents on the right path is the idea of receiving feedback sometime in the future.

Think of your child in the future asking you why you made certain decisions and choices about their lives. What do you think your child will say about the choices and decisions you made?

A happy childhood is not when a toddler or teenager tells you, because they depend on you for their survival.

Rather, it is that family man or woman who is happy to spend time with you and tells their child that they had a happy childhood.

Chapter 4

My child's requirements

This is where you start talking about what you think your child needs on their journey with you.

Find out from others if they agree with this book or your personal views.

Part 1: Uniqueness

How do I support my child's uniqueness?

Each child is a unique individual and as such requires to be cared for in a way that meets their specific requirements. You may notice by now that the word **'children'** has not been used in this book. It is imperative that parenting is tailor-made and not mass produced as one size does not fit all.

In treating your child as a unique individual, you will ensure that they are fed properly, given the right medical attention when required, and spoken to in a way that will promote their mental wellbeing.

You will nonetheless rely on your own experience and that of others or even use a style that has worked for another child of yours. If it is working and you are happy with the result, then there is no need to change. However, keep the notion of uniqueness in mind and make any necessary adjustments to suit each child.

Do not expect the child to be the same as their sibling because you are feeding them the same food and using the same parenting style.

Remember that your child is not going to share their place in life with any other. They are here to fulfil a role in society, and no one can take that away from them.

Encourage your child to strive for the best and support them; do not force them to become something you want them to be.

Part 2: Learning

How do I promote my child's learning?

Your child needs to learn to develop into a well-adjusted individual in adulthood. This involves different areas and stages. You will not bear the sole responsibility of ensuring that your child is given the opportunity to learn, others such as teachers, educators and coaches will have limited opportunity compared to a parent. You are the overall manager of all those who help your child along the way. It is your responsibility to ensure that anyone who gets the opportunity to teach your child meets your set expectations.

Learning is not limited to formal and non-formal education or teaching emotional and social interaction skills. Learning is a key component of child development. Every minute, every day, every situation presents the child with an opportunity to learn. Use of body parts, feelings, language, facial expressions, walking, reading, writing, telling the truth, and many more. You do not have to be an expert to understand how to promote your child's learning, neither do you need to be literate to get it right for them. One of the things a parent could do for their child's development is to **ensure that the child feels safe and secure enough to explore, play and ultimately learn.**

The details of how you support your child's learning on a day-to-day basis depend on your circumstances as a family and the society within which you live. **Ensure that you know your strengths and seek the best approach for your child when it comes to learning.**

The area of social interaction and emotional development need careful attention as this is what defines your child as a person (**refer to Chapter 3**). It helps if you continue learning as a parent. Learning does not have to take the form of a college course. There are many things out there that you can get into, it could be a hobby, trade, or lifestyle choice. What matters is that you are a positive role model in promoting your child's learning.

Part 3: Safety

How do I teach my child to keep safe?

Parents want their child to be safe and grow up without any major accidents. They accept that a child will fall a few times and experience cuts and bruises along the way. Although these make people sad when they occur, getting over them develops resilience.

The subject of safety includes giving your child appropriate guidance and setting boundaries that will keep them safe from significant harm. It is understanding that your three-year-old may not realise the hot pan on the stove is what burnt their hand last week. As a result, you will secure the kitchen and teach them that fire equals heat that can burn and continue to teach them until they get it. **Please don't leave your child to learn about safety, teach them.**

It is not likely that you will allow your child to be knocked down a few times by a lorry to learn about the dangers of crossing the road. You will go out with them as soon as they can walk and teach them how to cross the road until you are confident and have observed them do it safely on several occasions before you allow them out alone.

A child learns when they are taught, not when they are harmed. It is not possible to teach your child every safety trick on earth. Your role as a parent is to help your child build his or her confidence in the area of risk assessment so that they can assess whatever life throws at them and keep safe at all times.

Part 4: Honesty

How do I teach my child to live an honest life?

Be open and honest with your child to ensure that you do not leave them in doubt when you communicate anything with them. It is critical that your child can trust and rely on you for all their requirements. This way, your parenting will be effective as you will become a role model to your child. Being your child's role model is something that every parent must strive to achieve.

Let your child know when there is a problem if it will impact them. They do not need to know the exact details; they only need to be aware of the situation and this needs to be done in a way that is sensitive to their level of understanding. It helps if you can communicate appropriately with your child when sensitive issues are to be discussed.

Your child is not in competition with anyone so do not adopt a lifestyle that is beyond your means. If you need to save up for something that your child wants, speak about it honestly. If it is not within your financial means, say so. In the same way, if there is a problem within the family, ensure that the child's feelings are prioritised and inform them appropriately.

If there is no honesty or appropriate communication within your home, your child may pick up on this and suffer the impact. In their adulthood, your child may struggle to be honest with their partner, friends, child, or employers as dishonesty and lies becomes second nature to them.

Your child needs an honest environment where people communicate with each other appropriately.

Part 5: Stability

How important is a stable environment?

Promoting a stable and consistent environment for your child is key to them exploring and learning about life.

Humans generally thrive in a stable environment, be it the family home, school, or workplace. This is because we can concentrate on the task at hand and not worry about what is going on in the background. A stable environment helps a child feel safe and secure.

When a child wakes up to a constantly changing and inconsistent environment, it becomes difficult to continue any prior progress as they will be constantly thinking of what is coming next rather than playing and learning. The child may become anxious and unsettled and this makes it difficult for them to focus on being a child, which primarily is playing and learning.

Life is understandably challenging, and it may be that your family situation is constantly changing. This is where your resilience and determination as a parent becomes a lifelong lesson for your child. As you help your child to understand your family's circumstances, they will recognise your effort in constantly prioritising their wellbeing. Your child will appreciate and take cues from how you stay strong and not allow life to beat you down.

Promoting a stable and consistent life may not always be within a parent's control but ensuring a positive parenting experience is an essential part of a child's upbringing.

Part 6: Money

Do I need to teach my child about money?

Money and financial management play a significant role in every society. Lack of money can be an issue and having a poor relationship with money can negatively impact a person's wellbeing. The way to make and retain money is a topic that has been discussed in many books across the globe.

A parent does not need to read all these books or listen to the views and opinions of others before they decide to promote a child's economic and financial management skills. Most parents expect their child to be able to gain financial independence as early as possible in their adulthood. They may continue to support their child through further education or for various reasons if the means are available.

Promoting economic and financial management skills starts when the parent starts nurturing the child in a way that helps them develop the passion to learn and earn. Money is mostly made through economic activities either by direct or indirect involvement. A parent can use different routes to prepare a child for financial stability. For example, offer them good education or training, set up a fund for them, or give them start-up money or property.

Only a few parents go as far as discussing the subject and teaching their child about making and saving money. This may be because the parent is not good with money or has nothing to offer their child on the topic. If money is a topic you do not know about, learn about it. It could be the one subject that your child may see you learning during their upbringing. If you try to understand money and find that the subject is not for you, find someone to teach your child.

Money needs to be discussed regardless of how much or little there is within a family.

Part 7: Reflection

Why do I have to reflect on my parenting?

In addition to reflecting on your childhood and how your childhood experiences have shaped you as a parent, consider how day-to-day life is impacting your parenting abilities. You may have planned for a child and taken years to prepare emotionally and materially but as the months go by and you get to know your child, things begin to change. You get angry often and start raising your voice and ill-treating your toddler.

You may not be able to identify this unless you make a conscious effort to reflect on your actions. It may be one of the things you hoped to do differently because your parents used to shout and ill-treat you. It may be that times are getting hard, and you are not able to get by on your salary because of the expenses around the baby.

Reflection is one of the ways that a parent can identify which parenting practices are not working for their child. If you find that a certain parenting technique of yours needs to change, you can involve your child in the learning process. For example, asking your 3-year-old to go and sleep rather than settling them down into their bed. At age 10 when you reflect on their early years and realise that something you did when they were a baby has hindered their sleep patterns, talk about this with your child. This will enrich your child's parenting experience as they will learn that parents can make mistakes. **When you reflect on your parenting, you may identify your flaws and seek a remedy.**

You need to keep reflecting and adapting your techniques as a parent because your planned course of action may not always help your child. In other words, things may not turn out as you had hoped, and you may find yourself struggling with the basics of parenting.

Part 8: Support

Do I need support from others?

The level of support required by a parent depends on their strengths and limitations. A parent may live with their plight during difficult periods because they assume that the role they have taken on is meant to be difficult. **Parenting should not be a difficult time for any party involved** although it is expected to have several challenges. Childhood is meant to be an exciting time in the same way that parents are meant to enjoy their role.

When challenges arise, a parent needs to acknowledge the situation and be prepared to accept help. A parent cannot be told that they have a gap in their learning and offered a remedy when they do not recognise the issue. A parent needs to understand the value of a support system even if these are never used during their child's upbringing.

These support systems include books, direct or indirect assistance from friends and family in the form of emotional support, financial support, peer support groups, school parenting groups, online forums, and ad-hoc discussions with people who are knowledgeable about the subject.

Professionals are part of a parent's support network, and these can range from the day-care teacher to the pediatrician who monitors a child. It is okay to turn up and be told there is nothing to worry about than to be isolated and make mistakes that could easily be avoided. Do not hesitate to seek support as you may not always have the answer or necessary skills for a particular task.

A parent needs to maintain links with people who can offer support. This can be individuals or groups.

Part 9: Stress

How do I manage stress as a parent?

Life is not without its difficulties, and these become more complex when you are a parent. When you have a child in your care, it is not possible to ask for a break from certain roles. The child needs to be fed, clothed, emotionally supported, and kept safe. If you are in the position to rely on grandparents, friends, family, or paid caretakers, use them. A parent needs to maintain good health and general wellbeing.

In addition to the challenges that parenting will present, many other situations in life are likely to be stressful such as unemployment, ill health, relationship issues and bereavement. There will always be times where the unexpected or undesired will happen and this could have nothing to do with the child or be directly related to them.

A parent needs to prioritise their child's care amidst hardship and stressful times. Your child will not understand if there is no food because you do not have a job. They will not be happy if you are not emotionally available. In other words, **your child will find it difficult to smile at a crying mother.**

If you find yourself battling with depression, mental illness or addiction to alcohol or drugs, then you need to seriously consider letting someone else care for your child temporarily.

Your problems should not be your child's, it is okay to say you are struggling and ask for help.

Part 10: Endings

When does parenting end?

Understand and accept a child's development into adulthood because **childhood has an end.**

Parenting only exists when there is a child, and, in most societies, this is between 0-18 years, unless the child has special needs or additional requirements.

If you happen to be parenting an adult, then it is fair to say that you got it wrong.

A child who has received appropriate parenting is supported and encouraged to make the transition to adulthood. Such a person continues to learn about life and tends to make sound decisions that reflect all the important areas of life. They tend to understand that they are unique individuals, they keep safe, they are stable, honest, reflective, seek appropriate support, understand money, and embrace their transition into adulthood.

A parent who has done a 'good enough' job knows when the task is complete. Such a parent knows when to start preparing their teenager for adulthood and they ensure that the transition is smooth and sensitive to the requirements of their child.

Let go and start being part of their support network. Your 30-year-old with a child of his own does not need a parent, he needs a grandparent who can babysit and offer valuable parenting advice.

Chapter 5

Parenting discussion 2

Ask others what they think about the discussions in this chapter.

Part 1: Realistic Expectations

What if you are too late to change things as a parent?

As your child grows older, you become more knowledgeable about their needs and parenting in general and you start to identify things that will improve yours and your child's life. Making personal changes is difficult but parenting a child often involves other people who you could use to help you achieve your goals.

Making changes to your lifestyle is often a long and painstaking process. Some parents do not achieve their desired goal until after their child has grown into an adult. This does not mean that you have failed as a parent; you recognised the issue and genuinely made an effort to address it. Your child will see the effort you made and continue the journey of recovery in their adulthood. **You have taught them that life is a never-ending cycle of learning.**

If reading this book brings to light issues that you may need to change or improve with your parenting, please take a moment to reflect and talk to someone about this. Often when we find a fault or mistake, we want to see it fixed immediately or as fast as we can. However, parenting and most forms of human behaviour change takes time. When you learn something, and it becomes a habit, changing it could mean you have to learn to develop another habit or strategies to replace the old habit. Sometimes you can do this on your own or you may need someone to help you achieve your goal.

For example, if you have not been talking to your child who is now 16 years old about money and this book has brought that to your attention, you may have to give yourself time to teach them or you may need someone who has more knowledge to take the lead on this subject. You have to give yourself ample time to teach and your child the time to learn. You cannot put a timeline on this learning process, you need to be realistic about your expectations in regard to changing behaviour.

Part 2: External Issues

What is beyond my control as a parent?

As a parent, you may be faced with challenges from outside your home which may make it difficult or impossible for you to achieve your set goals.

For example, your child was abusing substance when he was 14 years old and you thought he was experimenting, and it was a phase that will pass. He is now 18-years-old, things have gotten out of control, and he needs to go to Court in 5 days for drugs possession. He blames you for everything and has asked that you stay away from him.

Life can present many challenges and we do not always have control over what is coming. Remember, we do not always get a second chance with the same child. You must accept that if you have not achieved what you would have liked to accomplish during their childhood, you have another chance in their adult life. You could put actions in place to ensure that the door is always open for them and if you have to knock on theirs every so often, that may be the way forward.

If you are fortunate to have another child in your care, let any previous unfortunate experience be your guide and ensure that the mistakes are not repeated. A mistake is only a mistake if you do not make a habit of the behaviour. You may be fortunate enough to get your second chance with a grandchild. Grab it and fulfil your role as a grandparent.

Good parenting is knowing that there will be many challenges along the way and being prepared to fix things and continue learning.

Part 3: Parenting Legacy

How will my child remember me?

Many people want to leave a legacy for their child, and they go to the end of their conviction to let everyone know what it is or how they intend to be remembered. There are many good examples of individuals leaving a legacy either by actively or passively working on it. Some may not have a legacy in mind but their efforts in parenting leaves a lasting impression on generations to come.

When I was writing this book, I asked two people about their parents' legacy. One said, "my father has not cared about me all my life", the other said, "my father has bought me two houses and two plots of land". The latter was 24 years old. She is pleased that her father was good to her, but she forgot that I was aware her father cut off her older sister at age 18 for marrying someone he did not approve of. No one in the family can speak to her sister whom the family was aware had struggled in her early twenties until she left their country.

A father cutting ties with an 18-year-old girl is not what most people would like as a legacy but unfortunately, this story will be told for generations if the older sister becomes a parent. We often expect to hear good things like a family business being passed on, higher education and perhaps an ostentatious lifestyle. Some parent's legacy to their child may include the skills training and life experiences that they offer the child to be able to live a happy and productive life.

The question at this point is what legacy did your parents leave you and what are you going to leave your child? Do you want your good name and traits to be spoken about for years to come? How then do you intend to achieve this, and will this be in the interest of your child? Whether you're aware of it or not, you will leave a lasting impression based on the choices and decisions you make as a parent.

Part 4: Professional Help

How do I know who to ask for help?

The childcare field has a myriad of professionals all of whom have their specialty. They include the pediatrician, nursery nurse, teacher, therapist, parenting coach, social worker, psychiatrist, support worker, youth worker, and the list goes on.

All these professionals have their place and time in a child's life. A child may need one or two, others benefit from having a team depending on their needs. Outside of this arrangement, many parents are left to decide which professional they need to support their child. Out of desperation and lack of understanding, some parents turn to the wrong professional for support.

It is difficult to tell if a professional is getting it wrong hence the need to ask them to explain their role and how they can help. In all professional fields, there are newly qualified people and there are the experts, and both can offer great support. Unfortunately, the childcare field is not spared when it comes to incompetency. There are some self-acclaimed experts who will confuse you with jargon and attempt a universal approach for every problem. This may be the nursery nurse who is trying to offer therapeutic support or the pediatrician who is playing a family support worker role.

Don't be shy to question your professionals to ensure that they are the right person for the job. Ask about the problem, understand the treatment or the support that is being offered.

If you get a treatment plan for your child and no one checks your parenting abilities, there is something wrong.

Part 5: Parenting Plan

What should a parenting plan look like?

Parenting a child is not like a puzzle that can be solved once. It is a cycle of life that requires ongoing attention, amendments, and reorganisation, hence the title of this book. You need to plan towards achieving a routine, or way of life, that gets you to an outcome or keeps you on your desired path.

For example, if your daughter does not share her thoughts with you, it can be disturbing because you want to know what your child needs so that you can offer her the right support. If you are aware that during her early years you could not bond with her because you had to work two jobs, then you will first need to focus on addressing that issue. You will work on making yourself emotionally available to your daughter by spending more time with her.

You may not hit the nail on the head initially but what matters is that you recognised that your daughter's behaviour is because you were not emotionally available.

Your overall plan is to have a close relationship with your daughter. You will find the little things that make this happen and work on those. The plan may include speaking to a professional, a friend or colleague for their advice. You could speak to as many people as possible to hear what they may do in your situation.

There are situations where the **plan** needs to be immediate. An example of this is a child abuse situation. If your parenting issue is a danger to your child then there is no need to have a **plan**, you may want to refer to the discussion on **Letting go**.

Change takes time and parenting is a journey, but it should not be a painful or difficult journey for you or your child. Talk to someone about your journey to ensure that you are travelling in the right direction.

Part 6: Life Story

How would you tell your child's life story?

If you must summarise your child's day to them every night, what would it look like? Let us start with your 3-year-old who is learning to understand language and still trying to have a dry day without wearing a diaper.

You woke up to a beautiful day, you had a little accident in bed, so we took out the sheets and made bubbles with the washing detergent. You asked for cereal, but you made a big mess and daddy had to clean-up, and you helped. Mummy got you ready for day-care and daddy dropped you off. Your teacher said you had a fun day, you played outside and ate all your fruits.

Mummy picked you up and brought you home. You had fun walking back home, you asked to play in the park, so mummy took you there for 30 minutes. We had dinner together, read a superhero story and watched monster trucks on the tablet. We had a good day.

Throw in some challenges such as, *we went to the shop, and you were crying because you wanted every toy you saw. I took you away from the toy section and we found you an Easter egg which made you happy.*

If your child is 10 years old, he/she can tell you how the day went and if they had some difficulty at school, you will be able to put a positive and re-assuring twist on it to **help close their day.** In the case of a 17-year-old, if you have been helping them with their life story from a young age, you are likely to continue having this dialogue to support them with their daily challenges.

Your child's story is not a random summary of what you think, it is the reality that they live every single minute.

If there are things that you would rather not include in the story, then you may want to ensure that they are not part of your child's reality.

You are not writing the story; your child memorises their story and that is their reality.

Part 7: What Happened to Us?

Where did the fun go?

The first year of a child's life is often filled with fun moments. Most parents can be seen getting down on their knees with the child, smiling, making facial gestures and are excited when the child smiles back.

We keep photographs on our mobile telephones, office desks and would post on social media so that everyone can see how much fun and happiness our child has brought to our lives.

We are excited and emotional when we leave our child at the nursery or school for the first time. We worry if we have left them with a safe person and rush back to collect our "buddle of joy".

We worry when our child has high temperature, and we are devastated when we need to take our child to the A&E for medical attention.

Suddenly, we are angry at them. We hate everything they do, and we criticize every choice or decision they make. We are constantly comparing them to others their age and some parents go as far as calling their own child "stupid and useless."

Pause, ask yourself what happened and how did we get here?

This perhaps is the time when you go back to **Chapter 3** to re-evaluate your own experience of parenting.

Why would you give yourself the permission to treat your own child this way?

Parenting is supposed to be a fun and exciting experience for you and your child. Find that balance and keep trying to make them smile back, even in their adult life.

Part 8: Empowering Your Child

How do I prepare my child for the challenges out there?

If your child was in a competition or an expedition, you will want him or her to do well, win, or have a great time. If it was an academic or sporting event, you will ensure that they train and prepare using the best equipment or material at your disposal. If it was a school trip or travelling abroad, you will do your own research and find as much information as possible for your child. You will want your child to be confident and believe in themselves. You will be their number one fan cheering them on and wishing them the very best.

The opposite of this will be knowing that your child has an event, expedition or competition coming up and doing all you can to sabotage them. The opposite of being your child's fan will be preventing them from getting the right training and support to be successful. It will be talking to your child in a way that will destroy their morale. It will be wanting to see your child suffer, loose the race, run out of money during their trip abroad and get used and abused by the people they encounter on their journey.

It is a tough world out there no matter which part of the globe that you may find yourself. If you are not running away from dangerous animals, you are probably worried about guns or perhaps not making it to your college of choice. There is always something that we aspire to achieve, and we most likely need to work for it.

From the first day of your journey as a parent, you will be preparing your child for an event. These may include the first day at school, the first attempt in a quiz, the encounter with a bully, or perhaps their final test in college.

Your language, your attitude, your aspirations for your child, your commitment to their day-to-day care, and your choices as a parent will determine whether you are a fan or you simply want your child to fail.

Be your child's number one fan and cheer them on to victory.

Part 9: Understanding Feelings

How do feelings impact on our lives?

We are emotional beings, and all our actions are aimed towards getting some sort of emotional response. We affect each other's feelings by our actions, and we respond or react to these actions. The nature of our journey is largely defined by our feelings and how we manage them.

Your child is born with the ability to experience all the feelings in the world but how they manage them depends on what they are exposed to or taught. One of our most common feeling is happiness which is often associated with laughter. In some households, you rarely see the parent laugh with their child, and this can be confusing for a child.

Some associate anger with loud outburst and destruction of property. Some teach their child to hit people whose actions makes them angry. As humans, we are supposed to know that when our actions cause others to be sad, we must stop whatever it is and apologies. The person who is not happy should be able to express themselves and try to change or avoid the situation from reoccurring.

These are some examples of feelings: fear, anger, sadness, shame, disgust, jealousy, happiness, love, surprise.

We react to fear to protect ourselves and we respond to love to express ourselves. Our knowledge and understanding of our feelings determine our character and defines who we are.

Lack of understanding of how to manage anger could make a person an aggressive individual which could sadly lead to hurting others and subsequently going to prison. As a parent, you have a role to play in how your child expresses and interprets feelings.

A parent needs to understand the impact and importance of feelings and guide their child on how to manage, respond, and react to them.

Part 10: Working Together

Do I need to listen to anyone?

We are at our best when we work together at work, within our communities, and as a world.

We share our knowledge, our resources, our expertise, and our drive to push forward as people. When one of us needs help, we go to their rescue and support them. When we see that someone is doing something wrong, we want to intervene and help them get it right.

We are there for each other in every aspects of our existence and our intentions are always pure. Yes, we can be our own enemies but that is not our nature as we often rediscover ourselves and stand up for what is right.

Our existence and quality of life depends on how we pass on knowledge from one generation to another. Every human needs to experience parenting before anything else.

Do we need each other when it comes to parenting? Should we be sharing ideas and comparing notes? Should we be having a conversation with the person next to us? Should we be speaking between

communities and amongst nations? What is the alternative if we want to get it right for our child? What other options do we have if we want to avoid mistakes?

The idea behind this book is to encourage you to ask questions and find as many answers as possible in your journey as a parent. Find answers from all corners of your community and across the globe if you have the means. Have a conversation about parenting, share ideas, Rediscover the strength in our communities, work together, hold each other accountable, question each other when we go off our course.

Our common quest is to provide our child with the best experience. We need to treat our child as a guest and offer them the best stay with all the bells and whistles every day that we have them in our Inns.

When parenting is understood, the journey becomes effortless and rewarding.

Enjoy your child.

Share

We have established from chapter 1 part 1 that 'good parenting' is within everyone's reach. We agreed that we may have different views on what we consider as important on our parenting journey.

We have different reasons and goals on our parenting journey and accept that the outcome will impact on our community and possibly the world.

This book talks about asking for directions from others which means that there are some great examples of parenting out there. You may be one of those whose journey has blessed you with extensive knowledge and experience. If this is you, then this book may validate your views and you may have more to add. **Share** your experience and offer others the answers and directions they need. When you get the privilege to share, please ensure that the recipients do not feel judged or controlled. ***You can show someone the right way, by telling them where you are heading and what your map says.***

Ask the questions and **share** your views. Keep asking so that you can have the opportunity to **share**. The more we **share** these positive experiences, the more likely they will resonate within our communities. We need people like you to **share** and even if it is the one thing that you think you got right, please **share**. For example, if the one thing you got right is potty training or encouraging a toddler to eat their vegetables, that is worth sharing to the world.

If you are unsure of your parenting and feel that you may need support, **please share**. It is only by telling the person at the crossroad where you are heading that they may be able to tell you if you are on the right track or you need to be on the other route. Sometimes, it may be a case of having to do a U-turn. There will be many challenges on your parenting journey and your goal is to ensure that you and your child have a wonderful experience.

If you feel the need to make changes after reading this book, do not worry. You can change directions or even make a U-turn. If you feel that you have made mistakes, then you are on the right track. Good parenting is knowing that there will be many challenges along the way but being prepared to fix things and continue learning.

Use your community to raise your child.

Or what do you think?